Questions for Couples

Deep Questions to Reflect, Building Trust and Regain Intimacy in Love Relationships

Margaret Douglas

Table of Contents

Introduction

C ouples seek advice from other couples. And while there are plenty of books out there that provide you with useful insight on how to answer this or that issue, how does one go about finding the right questions to ask?

By "right questions to ask" I am not referring to questions that will get you deep into the mind of your partner, although such questions are useful. Rather, I am referring to questions that help you get a clear sense of how your partner thinks about important things in life and what their attitudes are. In other words, questions that can help you better understand your partner's views during the early stages of relationship formation.

You see, though couples often come together initially due to some physical or emotional attraction they feel with each other (perhaps because they share similar backgrounds or because one or both of possesses social prowess), it is not only these qualities that make or break a relationship in the long run. Rather, it is how well the partners understand and deal with each other's attitudes and beliefs that determines the fate of the relationship.

In fact, one of the most important aspects of successful relationships is the ability to connect over topics considered important by each partner. Couples who share similar views about these "core" topics are more likely to stay together over time, whereas couples whose views are incompatible tend to live unhappy lives and eventually break up.

The purpose of this book, therefore, is to help you better identify your partner's "core" topics by focusing on questions that will get you thinking about these very issues. Of course, the specific questions you ask will depend upon your partner and what your relationship is like at the present moment. So in addition to suggestions for general conversation topics, you will also find specific questions for use when discussing each one.

Finally, you will find some recommendations on how to identify a topic as core by paying attention to how your partner reacts when certain topics are discussed around them.

For example, if your partner shows an intense interest in a particular issue that tends to upset them (such as if they cry during an argument over said issue), chances are that this issue is core to their life and that of their immediate family.

These discussions can be quite difficult and may leave you or your partner feeling a bit uneasy. Don't worry. It's worth it! In fact, this process is essential if you ever want to have a healthy relationship.

Couples who have a hard time talking to each other without getting upset, or those who have trouble communicating in general (often in stressful situations) may find some of the issues discussed below helpful. They can be considered core to the lives of most people, and therefore they will have an important impact on your relationships with loved ones. This does not mean that just because you think one or more of these questions are relevant you should ignore any other areas that trouble you and your partner – it is still important to find out where your spouse is coming from on all matters. But it does mean that if you're having trouble communicating with your partner, then these questions can be a good starting point for useful discussion.

This book is a compilation of questions on many topics related to how couples live their lives. Some are broader and some are more specific, but most will help you to talk with your partner about how you feel and think. Some of these questions have been around for years, while others were inspired by recent events in modern psychology research and literature. The point is that all of them have been selected because they make people think, and that's the key to a good conversation.

This book can provide useful insights in various situations: when you're picking up your partner at the airport, when you're shopping with your wife or husband, or even while sitting down with your kids at dinner. You could even use these questions for talking with friends, family members or other loved ones.

Most of these questions will help you to talk about the things that are important in your life. So keep them in mind next time you and your spouse want to have a meaningful conversation. It doesn't matter if one of you wants to talk about work and the kids while the other wants to talk about politics, religion, or philosophy — just start asking questions!

NOTES

Chapter 1:
Questions on Trust

T rust is a vitally important element in any healthy, loving relationship. Being able to trust your partner is the bedrock of the love you share. Without it, it's impossible for either of you to feel secure in your relationship.

But what does it mean to trust someone? To most people, trusting means believing that the other is being truthful and genuine in their actions, thoughts, and feelings - that they have your best interests at heart without an ulterior motive. But, in practice, this can be difficult to assess, especially in the early days of a relationship. And if you're wrong in your assessment and you trust someone who turns out to be untrustworthy, it can be devastating.

If you have difficulties with trust in your relationship and would like to build a greater sense of security and stability between you and your partner, try asking these questions for couples. They are likely to help you explore what it means to trust as well as define what makes you both feel comfortable with each other.

1. Have you ever felt like you shouldn't trust me?

Couples who trust each other have better, more stable relationships. When you trust your partner, you feel secure in the knowledge that they won't hurt you or let you down. And when they know that they're trusted, they feel better about themselves and their relationship with you. So, if you don't trust your partner, it's normal to feel nervous about what they're doing when they're away from you and whether they are faithful.

If that's the case for you, try to work out why – have there been times when your partner has behaved in a way that made you distrust them, or do you just get the feeling that they aren't as committed as you are? Be sure to talk to each other about how much trust matters to both of you and how important it is in a successful relationship.

2. What if my spouse was unfaithful?

This isn't a question about infidelity itself; rather, it's a question about one possible outcome if your partner were to cheat on you. Like many of the questions in this book (and in life), this one comes from "The Five Love Languages" by Dr. Gary Chapman. His theory is that there are five major ways to "speak" and show love to your partner – through words (quality time), acts of service (physical touch), receiving gifts (words of affirmation), quality time, or through physical touch or acts of service. Some people speak in all five languages; others speak only in one, two, three, while some speak only in the one language in which they're fluent.

3. What are the most important things I have to do to build your trust?

This and the following question (what are the most important things you have to do?) come from "For Better or For Worse: the Science of a Good Marriage" by Tara Parker-Pope.

The opposite of trust isn't expectation — it's betrayal. If you can't trust your partner, then all of the expectations in the world won't make a difference. What we want is for couples to have both trust and expectations; this allows them to work together toward common goals, both at home and in their relationship generally. If you want to build trust in your relationship, you need to find out what your partner needs. When it comes to building specific expectations, each of you has different expectations of the other, which can lead to disagreements (or worse) if you don't make a point of discussing them.

What are the most important things I have to do? What are the most important things I have to be? The answers will help you and your partner focus on your highest priorities for improving your relationship and keeping it strong.

Various therapists who work with couples often ask these questions of partners during an initial session.

4. Do you want to know more about my past relationships?

Couples don't have to share their entire past or even their present with each other. If you do feel like being open about things, then this question is a way to ask it gently and indirectly.

You should never force your partner to share things, but if you're talking about it and they seem hesitant, this question and the next provide ways to encourage your partner without being pushy.

5. What are the most important things I have to do to build your trust?

If you really want to build trust, you have to know what your partner needs. If your partner can't tell you what those things are, you need a more direct question like: what happens when my partner doesn't trust me? Those with a history of betrayal will struggle the most with this question because they may need to think about it carefully before they answer. So be patient while they work through their answer – if it's important enough for them to tell you, then it's important enough for you to wait for them.

5. What would help you feel more comfortable when talking about things in our past together?

This is the mirror of the previous question and one way of asking gently that might cause your partner less anxiety when you do choose to talk about past relationships.

If you do talk about your past relationships, and you and your partner are both willing, it's a good idea to keep a positive frame of mind. That means avoiding the past tense as much as possible when talking about interactions with exes. So say, "I love how so-and-so did this during our last encounter," not "I loved how so-and-so did this...(sniff)...last encounter."

7. How can I build my trust in you?

This question comes from "For Better or For Worse: The Science of a Good Marriage" by Tara Parker-Pope.

The opposite of trust isn't expectation — it's betrayal. If you can't trust your partner, then all of the expectations in the world won't make a difference. What we want is for couples to have both trust and expectations; this allows them to work together towards goals, both at home and in their relationship more generally. If you want to build trust in your relationship, you need to find out what your partner needs. When it comes to building specific expectations, each of you has different expectations for the other, which can lead to disagreements (or worse) if you don't make a point of discussing them.

If your partner has trouble trusting because of past relationships, then this question will help them start working through that issue with you and finding a way they can be more at ease taking new risks together.

8. What do you think we should do if we find out that someone is lying?

This question comes from research I conducted at the University of Toronto's Rotman School of Management and Baruch College in New York City. We found that couples with clear rules for what to do if one or both partners lie were more confident in their relationship and felt less distressed.

In fact, these clear rules for handling relationship problems were more important than both how many problems the couples reported and how satisfied they were in their relationships.

This question is a great way to add a little structure to your relationship and get your partner in the habit of working with you to figure out ways you can handle problems and work through conflicts more effectively.

The technique is based on research by Dr. John Gottman, considered the top relationship researcher in the world

9. Would you trust me if I asked a friend or relative to spy on you?

Asking someone to do this would be an act of distrust, so if your partner said yes, that would be a sign of trouble.

When you ask this question, you are thinking about what to do if your partner lies, so the answer is particularly important. Another reason for asking it is that if your partner says "yes" that would be an alarming indication that they do not respect your boundaries and privacy. Even if they say no, it still may mean they lie too much or feel comfortable doing things behind your back without telling you about them. Secrets breed lies and lying breeds secrets. It's a vicious cycle in relationships.

10. How would you feel about me having a close relationship with someone I work with?

Women tend to be more jealous when it comes to their partner having strong relationships with co-workers of the opposite sex, but men are nearly as bothered by opposite-sex friendships as they are by same-sex friendships — either way, they're concerned about losing their partner through a relationship with someone else. If the work environment is a source of stress in the relationship, then this question can help you or your partner work through the issue.

It's important to understand that no one person is the source of all of your happiness. It's okay to have outside friendships – it just needs to be without secrets. If you think about what makes close friends special, it's probably because they listen to you, tell you the truth about yourself and others. They help and support you, and they're always there for you. You want a relationship with someone at work with those same qualities.

These questions will help you and your partner work on trust issues together. This chapter is designed to help you understand what trust means, how to go about building it in your relationship, and how to deal with problems that arise due to or because of a lack of trust.

I've found that these questions work well during couples counseling sessions. I suggest that all of the couples I work with print out this list and discuss the questions together. It's also a good idea to keep answering them and discussing your answers with your partner even after you complete the exercise in counseling.

If you are having trust problems or have been hurt or betrayed by your partner, it's important to understand that trust issues often take time to heal. It's impossible to get over a past betrayal in one conversation. You and your partner need time and space for healing – plus, of course, good communication skills – so you can work through any problems together and come out stronger in the end.

NOTES

Chapter 2:
Questions on Communication

C ommunication is one of the most important aspects of a healthy friend or family relationship as well as significant other relationships because it fosters understanding between two people who are sharing their lives. But the importance of effective communication in a relationship is often overlooked, especially in the early days when you are caught up in the excitement of being with someone new who seems to understand you like no one ever has.

If you want to enhance your communication with each other and build a stronger sense of emotional intimacy, try asking these questions for couples. These questions are likely to help you explore your feelings about each other as well as enhance your ability to talk honestly and openly about any issues that might be holding you back.

Vital Questions for Couples to Discuss Together

1. What am I going to do about certain areas in our relationship? What are we going to do about them?

2. How should we communicate with each other?

3. What is one thing I need from you but we haven't done yet? That you feel we can't do yet? How can we work on these things together?

4. What is one thing that you as my partner needs from me but I haven't done yet? That you feel I can't do yet? How can we work on those things together?

5. How are you feeling about our relationship right now, right here?

6. What are the most important things you have to do to build trust in our relationship? What happens when we can't trust each other? What happens when trust is broken between us?

7. How is it different when we communicate about positive things versus when we talk about negative things in our relationship? In our lives in general?

8. What is one thing I do to make you feel less comfortable communicating with me and makes you feel less in control of the way we communicate?

9. How are you feeling about our communication right now, right here?

You and your partner need to create a plan for how you'll deal with areas of disagreement or problem behavior. You should agree to decrease your anxiety.

When there is a problem or an issue you see with your partner, have a plan in mind to address it with them. Plan on doing the following:

• Ask yourself if you are really upset. If so, ask yourself why this is upsetting you and what exactly about the situation might be causing it.

• Let yourself feel what comes up for you emotionally at the moment. Let yourself feel your feelings.

• Think about what you are going to do, say, or change in the situation or the way you react to it.

• Take a deep breath and step back from the situation. Rather than being sucked into reacting immediately, take a moment and consider how you might want to respond or act differently.

• Communicate with your partner (without nagging or yelling) in a calm manner about your feelings about the situation or behavior upsetting you. If possible, try to state your feelings in terms of feeling needs: "I felt disappointed when..." vs "You did such-and-such..."

• Communicate with your partner about what you are going to do differently.

• Agree on what you'll both need to do to make things different.

2. Ask how should we communicate with each other?

You and your partner should agree on how you can best communicate with each other, especially when an issue or problem needs addressing. You want communication with your partner to be as effective as possible so it can help you create a good relationship. You don't want communication to cause more trouble or conflict.

You want to the communication to be:

• Respectful

• Honest

• Focused on shared positive goals

• Based on the idea that both of you have good qualities and are trying to be a good people...not just that you have shortcomings.

• Based on the fact that your relationship is not about idealism but grounded in reality. This means it is based on shared interests, shared values, and what makes sense for the relationship. It's okay to have different opinions about some things as long as those differences don't threaten the core values or interests of the relationship: "We may differ about politics, but we can agree to disagree about that one topic without threatening our relationship."

• Based on the importance of the relationship to you and your partner individually. You care about each other and want to do what is best for yourselves and for the relationship. It's easier to focus on positive goals rather than negative ones.

3. What is the one thing that I need from my partner, but they haven't done yet? That they feel they can't do yet? How can we work on this thing together?

You should discuss what it will take for them to be able to create a sense of trust in the areas where you are struggling with trust. This may be about sharing personal information, behaving in certain ways, or in any other area you feel they need to build trust.

What can you do together to help the other person feel comfortable with issues that concern trust? What can you both do together as a couple that will help your partner trust you more? What is one thing that you want so badly that it creates doubt for them about your ability to handle whatever the issue is? (Maybe they don't want to see pictures of your ex, for example, but you don't understand why they would have a problem with it when it's just pictures?)

4. How is it different when we communicate about positive things versus how it is when we talk about negative things in our relationship? In our lives in general?

Again, this is a good question to ask if you are having problems in your relationship. If there are persistent issues that need to be addressed, pay close attention to how you and your partner communicate when talking about them. If you find yourself being harsh or using a lot of judgment, you might be dealing with some anger or resentment. If you find yourself coming across as overly accommodating, you may be suffering from fear and anxiety. If you find yourself avoiding the whole subject, there's a good chance that some anxiety is creeping into the relationship and causing stress.

Now how are you feeling about the relationship right now, right here? This is a more general question that might be helpful for you and your partner to keep returning to in the future. If you're worried about how your partner feels, ask about it! It might seem obvious from their actions (or lack of action), but sometimes we have a hard time articulating how we really feel about something in words.

What else could you bring up if it seems like they aren't doing a good job at communicating? What can you do together to improve this aspect of the relationship?

What are the most important things you have to do to build trust in the relationship? What happens when we can't trust each other? What happens when trust is broken? These questions will help you both understand the core issues of trust for your relationship. They can also give you an idea about what to do together if trust is an issue.

If your relationship seems relatively healthy, but there are still issues of trust here and there, it might be helpful for you and your partner to work on building trust in other aspects of your relationship. Perhaps you need better communication about how you're feeling or perhaps there's something they need to share more often.

This can be a long list, but it will help you both develop a better understanding of the issues that relate to trust. Use this list along with your own ideas about what is most important for you and your partner in order to improve this aspect of your relationship.

If something is an issue, but you don't see it here, feel free to add it. These things aren't to be taken too seriously. This is just meant to be a resource for you and your partner. However, I have seen these issues cause major problems in relationships. If any of these items are a more serious issue, consider working to solve them together.

You'll also want to pay close attention to the terms used to describe everything and everyone in your life. With constant negativity, the words used to label everything can be more black-and-white than need be. There's a good chance that such a relationship will fall prey to a particular kind of cognitive distortion, called, "all-or-nothing thinking."

When it comes to communicating about positive things and your relationship, keep an eye out for biased language. In other words, when you communicate with your partner about positive things, where are you coming from? Are your judgments and evaluations equally as harsh as they would be for negative things?

Looking into your mode of communication can help you spot issues that they may be having with their own communication. Try to inspect what you do and look for ways that your behavior could be affecting your partner's ability to communicate effectively with you. Are there times when you interrupt them? Do they ever feel like they can't express how they're feeling? Are there ways in which your attitude could be interpreted as controlling?

Asking yourself these questions can help you develop a better understanding of some of the factors that might be involved in your partner's inability to communicate freely and openly with you.

Other relevant questions: what is one thing that my partner does to make me feel less comfortable communicating with them? To make me feel less in control of the way we communicate with each other?

There are two sides to every communication, and even the most respectful, open communicators will have their fair share of issues with how they communicate.

Inspect what your partner does and look for ways that their behavior could be affecting your ability to communicate effectively with them. How are you feeling about our communication right now, right here?

In this chapter, we've covered a lot of areas where trust can be built, and issues of trust can occur. You want to consider how your relationship is coming along in terms of the way that you communicate with each other on a daily basis. This is the basis for all of your relationship.

Your answer depends on where you are right now, and it's important to acknowledge that you will have good days and bad days. That's not a problem – all relationships go through ups and downs. Just try to answer these questions as honestly as you can, even if it takes more than one try. You may want to discuss your answers with your partner to extend the conversation.

When thinking about communication in your relationship, pay attention to how you both feel about the way that you communicate with each other on a day-to-day basis. Is there a difference between how you feel about communicating in general and how you feel when you two communicate specifically?

These questions are designed to help you and your partner communicate in an effective way that will build the trust in the relationship. They are also designed to help you both build a better understanding of how each of you impact the other's ability to communicate effectively with each another.

That said, there is a wide variety of communication styles out there, so don't feel boxed into these questions if they don't work for you and your partner.

NOTES

Chapter 3:
Questions on Fun

F un and playfulness are often overlooked in relationships, especially in the beginning when you're more focused on falling in love and discovering who you are.
But it's important to remember that all relationships need to
have moments of fun and playfulness to make them strong
and healthy, because the love you share is enriched by the
joy you have just being together.

If you want to bring more fun into your relationship, try using these questions for couples. They are likely to help you
explore what it means for you both to have fun together as
well as what makes each of you feel playful around each
other.

Use these questions at any point during your relationship
they're especially helpful when getting to know each other
better. It's important to have fun with each other, so have
fun answering these questions!

1) What do you like most about being with me?

This question is a great way to get things started. It helps you
focus on the good, which will naturally lead into deeper conversation. The key to having good playfulness in your relationship is having a sense of humor about yourself and each
other.

2) What does it feel like when we are enjoying being together?

What actions do you take? What do you say? How do your bodies move? This question will help you focus on physical playfulness in particular, which can be important if you want to have more physicality in the relationship.

3) How do you like to spend time by yourself?

How do you like to spend time with me? It's important to know that the playfulness and fun in your relationship isn't just about making sure each person is happy all the time. It's about acknowledging each person's separate interests, activities, and joys, as well as bringing these things together.

This question helps you understand what brings joy into your own life and makes it a question of sharing that joy with each other. When that happens, it allows you both to be more playful with each other while still maintaining your own individual characteristics. Which leads us nicely to the next question.

4) What do you like best about me?

This question can be a bit more difficult, because you might not always know how to answer it. You might feel like there isn't much to say or that your love for each other is already apparent. But trust me, this question is a great way to bring deeper conversation and fun. Try answering from different perspectives, such as, "What do you appreciate about me?", "What do you find attractive about me?", or "How have I grown as a person?" You may also want to ask each other questions that allow you both to put yourselves in the other's position for a change.

5) When do you feel most playful with me?

This question is a great follow-up to the previous question. It requires that you think about what it feels like when the two of you are being playful together. A lot of people find this question hard, because they don't believe they have been as playful as they could or that their partner doesn't have the same ideas about playfulness as they do. But focus on what does feel fun to you, and try to understand why some it makes you want to be more playful with each other. Then, think about answering this next question...

6) What do you think I might appreciate about being with you?

If you want to see more fun in your relationship, this is an important question to ask. It requires that each person focus on the other person's perspective, allowing for a deeper understanding. If you don't feel like you know how to answer the question, ask your partner what it might feel like being with them. This will give each of you some insight into how the other person feels.

7) What physical activities do we enjoy together? This is a great question if you're trying to bring more physicality into the relationship. Especially if you aren't used to being physical or don't have a lot of shared interests, this question can be a good way to come up with new ideas of things you can do together. Even if you already know what kinds of physical activities the two of you like, answer the question again. This time, think about it from another person's perspective. What would they find fun and exciting about the two of you being physical together?

Now we move on to some questions more focused on the relationship as a whole...

8) How do you feel when we're having fun?

This is an important question because it's important to remember that each relationship is different. Some people don't feel much of anything when they are enjoying themselves, while others feel a lot of emotions. Some people really notice a change in their body, while others don't. Or maybe you really get into the fun and are more playful than normal. This question will help you understand your partners feelings about being happy and having fun together.

Because each relationship is different, each relationship needs to find its own balance of fun and serious talk. If you don't have time for deep discussions every day, that's okay! For some relationships, it might be more important to set aside some time on the weekend for getting to know each other better, while other relationships thrive on constant communication.

Whatever you need to make your relationship work, you can find ways to add playfulness throughout the week. Maybe try to ask a question during a fun moment together!

For some questions, you may need to think about your answers for a while and spend some time together reflecting. If this is the case, feel free to write down your answers and share them with each other later!

It can be hard for us to remember why we fell in love with each other in the first place. And sometimes we get so caught up in day-to-day life that we don't remember to appreciate what makes our relationship special. That's why it's important to take some time to think about these questions and what they mean for you and your partner. If you're constantly communicating with each other, you'll stay connected during the fun and the hard times. And even if things change, it can help to remember why you fell in love in the first place!

After answering these questions about fun and playfulness with each other, take some time to discuss what it was like to answer them. What did you learn about each other? Did one of your answers surprise the other? Did anything you said make you feel differently about each other, or about your relationship?

Now it's time to get playful!

NOTES

Chapter 4:
Questions on Respect

W hen a man is motivated by a desire for respect, he will often give you everything you ask, no matter how unreasonable it is, and no matter whether you deserve it or not.

Respect is the outward expression of approval; it can be given only by those who have control of some kind over the person who receives it. "Give me respect" means "Make me feel important." To inspire respect in others we must convince them that we are superior to them in some way. But their position in relation to us is not important; what matters is the way they feel about themselves compared with how they think we feel about ourselves.

This is why we respect those who are self-assured and we usually feel contempt for those who have no doubts. In other words, it is not so much their positive qualities that inspire us to give them respect as the absence of negative characteristics.

When people are aware of their weaknesses, they automatically become unsure of themselves. They want to cover up their inadequacies but do not know how to do so. Though they fear the judgment of others, they can never be quite sure what other people really think of them. In this situation there is only one way for them to be accepted, and that is by constantly trying harder than everyone else. There are only 10 questions important for you and your partner to answer regarding respect:

1. What do you think makes you a better person than me?

To answer this question, you must first ask yourself the following what good qualities do I have that my partner does not? What are the things that I would like to change in my partner—the things that prevent him from being as good a person as I would like him to be?

When a person realizes that his partner is more talented or better at something, he feels inadequate and inferior. And when a person feels inferior toward someone else, he will try to develop feelings of jealousy or hostility so strong that they overpower his feeling of inadequacy. But if your partner has something you want and you don't think you can get it by competing, you will feel tremendous resentment rather than jealousy. Resentment is a powerful emotion that can be used to control and dominate others, and it is one of the most dangerous feelings that can develop in a relationship.

Those who ask this question are often not really interested in the good qualities or abilities their partners possess, but

44

instead they are looking for a feeling of security in relation to something they consider a weakness. For example, if your partner is very generous with her time and energy and knows quite a few people, you might worry that she will find someone else who will take up more of her time than you do.

2. If I tried to behave the way you want, what would stop me?

When a person feels guilty, inadequate, or inferior, he usually has a kind of inner barrier that prevents him from acting the way he wants to. This barrier is like a series of self-imposed negative attitudes that give him something to feel guilty about even before he does anything wrong.

For example, an individual who feels guilty when he shows anger will make sure that his partner is never angry at anybody else; but whenever she gets angry with him, she will be expressing mistrust or resentment because he had thought of doing something she would not have wanted him to do.

People use their personal feelings as an excuse for not taking responsibility for themselves and their relationships. They feel that it is not their fault if their partners don't behave the way they want them because they are naturally good people and would never hurt anyone. But in relationships, they allow themselves to get upset even though they know that at any moment they can change their feelings. The idea that they have done something wrong becomes an excuse for getting upset and blaming others for their negative feelings.

3. What makes a man friendlier and more responsible than he actually is?

When people feel guilty or resentful toward someone for some reason, they act friendlier toward him than he deserves. This is called "being nice." While this may seem like it is being friendly to the other person, it is actually something very different. When a person sees someone of the opposite sex who attracts him, he will usually act in a way that indicates attraction. If he is friendly or nice to her, then he will assume that she will feel good about herself and want to be closer to him because she will think she is so desirable. In fact, if a woman feels attracted to a man and wants to be close to him, she will act more attractive toward him as soon as possible.

Women are usually more direct and open about their feelings than men; they don't have as much trouble being open and honest with their partners. This is why men, when they are un-confident and insecure about their attractiveness, will often try to act friendlier or nicer to the women they would like to be close to than is necessary or justified. Men will show off their ability to be friendly and supportive by offering favors that are not really needed, since they don't feel secure that the woman in question would want them for herself.

4. What can I do that will make you feel that my presence raises your status?

People are so used to acting in a certain way around others that they don't realize how others feel about them. Even though your partner might be loyal and loving, she will still see that something is missing in you, such as more money or better looks. If you can think of a way to act that will make her feel that your presence is not only comfortable but actually elevating her own status, then she will be more attracted to you.

5. How does a person who is incompetent and irresponsible act when he wants to make others feel good about themselves?

Even though many people are not in touch with their own feelings, they usually know if their actions make them feel good or bad about themselves. This is why incompetent people often act in ways that make others feel guilty or ashamed.

They do things that cause them to feel good about themselves by making others feel bad. If a man does something wrong, he will try to make others feel responsible. For example, if a man is poor and can't take his wife out on weekends, he may try to convince her that it's unfair for him to have all the responsibility for supporting the family while she doesn't have any at all. He makes himself seem like the victim, and she feels guilty for not being more supportive.

6. How can I improve my relationships with those people who are already friendly toward me?

If you want to improve your relationships with people who are already friendly toward you, then make an effort to be with them more often. People who are already friendly toward you may feel honored if they can be around you, and this would improve the relationship. If you have people in your life that like being around you, see if there is some way that the two of you could become closer.

7. What emotions do I feel towards the persons who are already friendly toward me?

If you have people in your life who are already friendly toward you, look at what emotions you feel toward them. Are you happy they think so highly of you, or do you feel some jealousy that they have a better relationship another person than you do? If you can be honest with yourself about your own feelings, then it will be easier to find ways to fix these relationships by addressing such issues. If you are close to becoming friends with someone and still harbor jealousy or envy toward them, it will be hard to make your relationship solid because you will always feel like they have something you don't. This isn't the way a good friendship should be, and it's better to address your feelings head on.

If there are people who dislike you, do not immediately assume that they have valid reasons. Someone who dislikes you might simply resent something about your personality. Sometimes people try to improve themselves by learning about how other people behave.

7. How can I be a better person if my friends try to make me feel that I can improve my status?

If your friends were to try to make you feel that you have improved your status by making a lot of money, getting published, or achieving something important, then it is possible that you will change in the way they want. But if your friends are honest and accept you as you are, there is no way that they will try to make you feel like this. So this question requires some serious concern on our part.

If your partner has asked any of these questions about herself—questions about her good qualities and desirable characteristics—we can assume that she is aware of something good about herself and probably has a few qualities that attract people to her.

8. How would you like me to act for the two of us to get along better?

If your partner has asked you this question, she probably feels that you are not as close to her as she would like you to be. She will feel very frustrated if she feels that you are not close enough because she has the deep feeling inside that there could be something great between the two of you. The chances are good that there is something negative between the two of you, but it is better to look at what's positive as well.

9. If people were constantly trying to put me down, what can I do about it?

Many people have the idea that if someone were to try to hurt them or make them feel bad about themselves, they would act right away to defend themselves. But in reality, if someone always makes you feel bad, you will probably just keep trying to avoid that person. For example, if your partner doesn't want you in his life because he doesn't like himself and can't accept his own mistakes, then he will try to get back at you by making you feel guilty for something. Then when you are feeling guilty and insecure about yourself, he will start telling you that it is your fault for not being supportive enough because he needs your understanding.

10. How can I give people more respect than they give themselves?

If you can figure out how to do this, you and your partner will be able to make the most of the relationship. If your partner feels that you respect him more than he respects himself, he will probably feel much better about himself.

These questions are designed to help you respect each other as couples. If you believe that your partner has good qualities, you will want to be close to him. If you are interested in improving your relationship, you can begin by finding out what is holding you back from getting closer to each other.

NOTES

Chapter 5:
Questions on Quality time

Q uality time is one of the most important aspects of a relationship. It doesn't have to be fancy or expensive. All you need is each other; and sometimes that's all you need to make things seem right in the world again.

Grab some popcorn, settle down for a cozy night in, and ask each other these questions to get things going! You'll be surprised at what you learn.

1. What do you enjoy doing together?

This question is extremely open-ended, and it will allow both parties to talk about their favorite things to do as a couple. It can be as simple as walking around the block or going out for a milkshake, but it's rare that couples get the chance to discuss little joys like this!

2. Where would you like to go someday?

This question is a good one for those who are married and have already been on various vacations. It's also perfect for those who simply want to travel and need some inspiration! Asking each other where you've always wanted to go is a great way to have fun dreaming and planning your future adventures together.

3. What is your favorite memory of us together?

This question is all about reminiscing. It will allow both partners to share the funniest or most touching moments of your
time together. Even if you've heard these moments a million
times before, asking this question again is a great way to
spark renewed joy and laughter in your relationship!

4. How would most people describe the two of us as a couple?

Couples rarely take the time to stop and think about what
others think of them as a unit. This is an opportunity for you
both to step back and see how others see you, which can provide insights into the type of people that the two of you are
as a couple!

5. Who is the most important person in your life, besides
me?

This question is all about getting better acquainted with each
other. It will allow you to see how important your partner is
to you outside of the relationship. Often, it can spark conflicts because one partner may not appreciate the amount of
time the other spends with family or friends. When dealing

with this issue in a relationship, it's important for both partners to be open and honest so that these types of conflicts can be addressed early on before they get blown out of proportion.

6. What do you like most about being married?

This question is a fun one that will allow each person to reminisce about the reasons why you got married in the first place. It will provide renewed joy and reason to be grateful that you're together. It's also a good tool for those who may have been together for so long that you've forgotten what you saw in each other in the first place.

7. If I could change one thing about myself, what would it be and why?

This question can ignite a firestorm of honesty which is always needed between partners. If your partner says that he wishes he were taller or she wishes she had bigger boobs, it will make you think about your own self-image and how those things impact the relationship as a whole.

8. Why did we decide to get married in the first place, and how is it working out so far?

This question can be extremely important because it will allow you to see what the big picture in your relationship when you got married. It may reveal that you both expected very different things from marriage, which may lead to an unexpected conflict. It can also provide a good way for both of you to reflect on your individual expectations of marriage before it became a reality.

9. What is the best thing about having kids?

If you have any little ones running around, this question will generate some serious laughs (and probably a few tears). Not only is it a great way to enjoy a night in as parents if you have the kids at home, but it can also be a good way to see just how much the two of you have in common. If your opinions are polar opposites on this topic, some tension needs to be addressed!

10. Where do you see us in five years?

This is another question that allows both partners to step back and look at the big picture. It will allow both parties to reflect on where they see themselves and their relationship going forward. It's also a great tool to provide perspective on how you've both grown in your relationship and whether or not it's heading in a positive direction.

These questions are all great tools to help you get to know each other on an intimate level. They'll spark discussions and allow the two of you to look at your relationship from a different perspective. If you and your partner can answer them together, it will provide a safe place for both of you to share some vulnerability that will strengthen your bond as a couple.

NOTES

Chapter 6:
Questions on How to fight fair

I n order to fight fair, you need to have a clear understanding of what is it you are fighting for and why. What is it about the situation that upsets you? Is this an issue that can be resolved through constructive discussion? Do you want to make your partner aware of something they do not realize? Are you trying to change a current behavior pattern by putting pressure on the other person?

Don't focus solely on what's wrong in your relationship. Focus also on the positive aspects and possible solutions; there might just be ways in which both parties could compromise and work together. Whatever your goal is when fighting, be fair and try not to put blame or throw judgmental criticism at each other. This will only cause the other person to react defensively. If your partner is capable of accepting responsibility for his or her actions, you can actually make them feel more secure. If your partner is defensive, try not to take it personally. This is a sign that you have done something wrong and need to correct it.

When fighting fair, remember to listen and understand what the other person has to say before you continue with what you were saying. You may be surprised to find that the root of the argument was not even related to what you originally thought. We often enter into arguments thinking we know exactly why because we tend to focus on ourselves—our own feelings, beliefs and wants—rather than our partner's thoughts and feelings.

Here are questions for couples to ask each other. Use these questions to guide your discussions and try not to get into the same arguments using the same words, each time.

1. What do you consider to be a healthy relationship?

A healthy relationship is one in which the couple has empathy towards each other. They listen to each other and appreciate what they do for each other. They have a sense of mutual trust.

2. What is love? How do you show your partner that you love them? Love is an action, not a feeling. Showing your partner that you love them means taking the time to do little things for them. It could be as simple as doing their laundry or giving them a foot massage.

3. What does intimacy mean to you in a partnership/marriage/relationship and how can we create more intimacy in ours?

4. What is a healthy balance of individuality and togetherness?

5. What would it take for us to move forward and make the changes we want to make in our relationship?

6. Do you think we can make these changes or is it time to move on? (If one or both don't want to work on things, then it's time.)

7. What is respect and how can we show respect in a healthy relationship?

Respect is treating each other with dignity and kindness, no matter what the situation - right or wrong. This includes having patience with one another, listening to each other and considering what the other partner has to say before responding instead of reacting defensively.

8. Why do we have conflict in our relationships?

Conflict occurs whenever there is a difference of opinion or point of view. The main source of conflict is when there is disrespect, or one partner feels as though the other does not appreciate him/her or care about his/her feelings. This can happen when we are under stress, tired or frustrated. One way to prevent this from happening is by being genuine with your words and actions; in other words, mean what you say and do what you say you are going to do!

9. How did our family influence how we handle conflict and deal with each other as adults?

Our families, whether they be immediate or extended, have an immense impact on who we are as individuals. Perhaps one or both of you had a parent who was overly strict and demanding, or perhaps one of your parents was always yelling at you to do well in school (or did not encourage you enough). You felt as though you could never get enough praise. Your family taught you how to deal with conflict in an unhealthy manner; the sooner we learn to deal with conflict positively, the better off we will be in our relationships.

10. How did growing up together or apart affect how we relate to each other as adults? (separated couples only)

It is important to remember that your past does not have to determine your future. When people who are abused and/or neglected come together in a new relationship, they often find themselves repeating the same unhealthy patterns of communication and behavior that they experienced in their families. This is because they had no one in their lives telling them at an early age that what was happening was wrong, and no one teaching them how to deal with conflict in a healthy way.

This is a big reason why people leave their partners; most of the time, it is not because they don't love them or want to be with them but because they can't get out of those unhealthy patterns of behavior and/or they can't stand to see the pain in their partner's eyes.

11. What does intimacy mean to you in a partnership/marriage/relationship and how can we create more intimacy in the relationship?

Intimacy means closeness and connectedness. It is not, as many people think, sexual activity. Too often, couples wait to discuss important issues until after they have had sex. This only allows the issue to fester and grow into something bigger than it was when it started. If you really want a healthy relationship, you have to make time for intimacy.

12. How do we go about setting up boundaries and rules to promote a healthy relationship?

It is important that each person be clear with their partner what their boundaries are and that they respect one another's boundaries as well as those of their extended family and friends! Role-playing is a great tool for helping couples set up boundaries in an easy way that does not hurt anyone's feelings!

13. How do you feel about money? Do you think that it is important to share financial responsibilities?

Money can be an issue in any relationship. Many people never get over their resentment and anger toward their parents for the way they handled money when they were growing up. Some people use money to keep score, while others are afraid that if they have too much, their partner will leave them or take it away, etc. If money is a problem for your partner, then you must deal with it and find a way to make the other person comfortable with the situation!

10. What are your life goals for the next 20 years?

Knowing where you want to be in 5, 10 or 20 years is an important part of any relationship. If both partners share the same goals, then it can help build a rewarding and loving relationship. If one person has no interest in reaching their dreams, then they may resent their partner for holding them back.

You might want to take turns answering the questions. As you talk, listen for underlying feelings and unspoken expectations that need to be understood and resolved. Remember to focus on feelings and not on right/wrong, good/bad or whose fault it is. Keep the discussion focused on issues and not your partner or yourself.

Also note that some of the questions above will be more relevant for couples who have been together for a longer time than those who have been together for just a few months. After all, there is a lot to learn about each other during courtship, but there is even more to learn about each other after many years of marriage. You will want to add more questions based on your situation and experience as well as any concerns you might need to discuss with each other.

It is important that the questions not offend, upset or otherwise trigger your partner in an unhealthy way. If you notice that a question upsets your partner, it is best to replace it with another question.

If you use any these questions in a discussion, record the responses recorded for future reference. It will take time and requires patience but it is possible for both of you to learn and grow from the process of fighting fair. Once fighting fair is understood by both parties, it will only become a matter of time before you realize how much progress you have made together as a couple.

NOTES

Chapter 7:
Questions That Make you Think

S ometimes, our days are so busy that we barely have time to think. And when you're in a relationship, it can be hard to find moments where you can see the big picture and make decisions together. But it's important to set aside some time for this because it will have a huge impact on your relationship. Start by thinking about how you and your partner feel about each other right now in general and then narrow it down to how you feel about specific things like communication, sexuality or relationships with parents and friends. The more you know about each other, the easier it will be to discuss the issues that come up along the way.

When answering these questions about how you feel in general, think about everything, including the little things. Rate your feelings on a scale from 1 to 10. And if you need help deciding how to rank each item, ask yourself these questions: is this feeling something I am totally comfortable with? How much do I support it? Does this feeling make me want to change anything in my life?

To get started with these questions, ask yourself:

1. Am I making a decision about my health because I understand my options?

This question will help you focus on whether or not you really understand the options that have been presented to you. If your decision isn't based on understanding and knowledge, it will be hard for your partner to trust that you're making the right decision for yourself and the relationship.

If you need more information, ask your doctor or a trusted family member or friend to help explain things in a way that makes sense to you.

2. Am I making the decision that is best for me?

This question will help you focus on what's most important. It will help you think about your wants and needs, and the wants and needs of your partner. It will also make sure you're not being influenced by things that have nothing to do with your health or treatment plan.

If your decision isn't what's best for both of you, talk with your doctor or a trusted friend so they can help to make sure it fits with all the other parts of your life.

3. Have I thought about how my decision will affect my partner?

You may feel that you're making a decision for yourself and not your partner, but your partner's opinion matters. They have the right to decide how they feel about your decisions and whether or not they are okay with it. If you aren't thinking about how your decision will affect them, it might not be the best decision for either of you.

If you don't know how your partner feels about what you're doing or would like to include them more in this process, talk with them.

4. Have I explained the treatment decision to my partner?

You may not want to tell your partner every detail about the problem, but it is important to talk it over with them. Your partner may be able to help you understand things like cost, the process of treatment, and the potential side effects. Plus, you might find out that your partner is uncomfortable with a certain choice or may have questions of their own.

If they don't understand what you're doing or don't approve, don't be afraid to talk about their feelings and try to come up with something that works for both of you.

5. Will my decision be good for me in the long term?

This question will help you focus on what will happen after your treatment. It will make sure that you're not just thinking about what happens immediately, but also down the road.

Keep in mind that health problems change over time, so you may need to get more treatment or have a different option later on.

If you feel like your choice doesn't address future issues, talk with your doctor, a friend or partner about it.

6. Have I thought about how this decision fits into my life as a whole?

Think about things like school, work plans and social activities that are important to you. Are there other things in your life that may make this decision harder to accomplish?

For example, some of the decisions you might need to make are hard if you have a job, kids, or a family. But if your decision fits into all the parts of your life, it will be easier to follow through.

If this decision doesn't fit in with the rest of what's going on in your life, however, talk with your doctor or trusted friend about it so they can help you find a different option.

7. Do I understand how to take care of myself if I decide to have treatment?

Some treatments can be hard and may need special follow-up care. It's important that you know what your treatment will be like, who will help you with it, and what kind of follow-up care you'll need.

Sometimes this information is hard to find, so talk about what kinds of things you'll need to do after the treatment is over.

8. Am I sure about my choice?

Ask yourself if there are any doubts in your mind about making a decision now. If you're not sure whether to have treatment or not, you should talk with your doctor or someone you trust. After a while, decide if you'll have treatment or not. If you decide to wait for now, add the following question to your list:

9. Have I talked about my decision with family and friends?

If there are things in your life that are important to other people (like your friends, family, and religion), involving them can make things easier. It can also help with making big decisions (like whether to have treatment or not).

How do you get started? You may feel a lot of pressure to "just get started." But take it easy because you're the one who is going to be doing all the work, and none of it has to be done all at once.

Next, follow these seven steps:

1. Make a list. Write down the things that are important or interesting for you at this point. Your list could include things like your disease and its symptoms, treatment decisions, or important life questions (like what kind of work you want to do or where in the world you want to live).

2. Make a timeline. When are you going to think about your choices? Maybe you want to make a list of questions at the beginning of each week, or maybe you want to talk things over with your partner once a month. Then decide when you're going to review and update your list so that it's always ready when you need it.

3. Pick up the pace. As time passes, some of these questions may feel less important or urgent, so don't stress if it takes longer than expected to finish your whole list; just do what works best for now and adjust as needed later on.

4. Keep it all in one place. If you're going to have more than one list, keep them together so all your questions are easy to find. Maybe you want to keep a notebook with your list of questions or put your questions on sticky notes that are easy to move around.

5. Share the load. It can be good to talk about big issues with friends and family who care about what happens next or who can offer a different perspective on your future plans. But remember that it's your decision so don't let anyone else make it for you, especially if they don't know what's best for you or your relationship.

6. Give yourself some space. It can be hard to think about a lot of things all at once, and you might find it easier to think about some parts of your list one at a time. If that works for you, schedule time: I'll work on my list on Mondays and Wednesdays from 12:00-1:00 (or whatever works best for you).

7. Take charge of your own health care by getting the information you need and make sure that all your questions are answered before making a decision.

After answering these questions about your health, feelings and views about relationships and life in general, take some time to discuss what it was like to answer them. Get an idea of your partner's responses and how those views are different or similar to yours. Then put these questions away for a little while and work on other exercises.

While you're both working on other exercises, stop thinking about the list of questions and try to let go of whatever feelings or thoughts they brought up. When you're ready to move back to this list, go through them one at a time so that your partner has a chance to answer them too.

If you find yourself getting upset as you think about answering these questions, try breathing slowly (inhaling and exhaling for five counts each) until you feel more relaxed. If that doesn't help, try to distract yourself by thinking pleasant thoughts or do something that takes your mind off the stressful situation. For example, you might try talking to a trusted friend or doing things you enjoy that don't involve thinking about your health.

Making the decision: finally, when you reach the point where you feel ready to make a decision (and have made sure that all your questions have been answered), consult with someone who has gone through this process and whose opinion you value. Choose someone unbiased and supportive of your decision, if possible. This person can be your counselor, doctor, a friend or family member. They will help you think about your situation and get a fresh perspective on the issue.

When you're ready to make a decision about your health, it's important to make it on the basis of good information and not just strong feelings. Use the following questions to guide you through the decision-making process. These questions are designed for after you have made some choices about treatment options and want to make sure your decisions are based on solid information and good thinking.

When dealing with important issues like these, it may be hard for you to keep your focus on the right things. If that's the case, take a break and come back to the questions when you feel ready. Or talk with someone you trust who can help to keep your thoughts grounded or find another way to get through it.

NOTES

Chapter 8:
Questions on Conflicts with In-laws and Extended Family Members

Relationships with in-laws and extended family members can be a source of stress and frustration for everyone involved. In this chapter, we'll look at the root causes of these conflicts, potential solutions to reduce future conflict, and learn how to have better communication with each other.

Are you interested in knowing how to deal with your spouse's in-laws or extended family members? Take a look at our list of 10 questions for couples!

1. Does you feel as strongly about the issue as I do?

This question could be the most important one on the list. It is vital to figure out if your partner is as invested in solving the issue as you are. Perhaps you have differing opinions on dealing with certain conflicts. Discuss these differences and how you can come to a solution that works for both of you instead of going your separate ways.

2. How would you describe your relationship with my family members?

Sometimes your partner may be unwilling to open up about his or her family relationships due to various reasons, including fear of creating conflict or embarrassment, or anything else that may cause distress. Be patient and find a quiet time to have a non-confrontational conversation with your partner where you can discuss your concerns.

3. How does you feel when around my family members?

Sometimes conflicts between family members may be related to differences in cultural upbringing or opinions. For example, one spouse may have limited contact with his or her parents due to differences in religion or lifestyle, while the other one maintains frequent contact and visits often. If you ask this question and find that your partner is uncomfortable when you are around their extended family, it could be because he or she feels embarrassed about the differences in opinion, lifestyle or culture between the two families.

3. What would you like to see happen in our relationship with family members?

The answer will let you know what your partner thinks about the current state of his or her relationship with his or her relatives. You can then work together to find a solution that is mutually beneficial for everyone involved.

4. What have you done so far about this issue?

If your partner feels as strongly about the issue as you do, it may be because he or she has already brought it up in conversation with family members before and even come up with a solution to fix it. If this has happened before, make sure to understand what steps have been taken so far and if they were successful.

5. What will you do if I don't want to deal with the issue anymore?

It is important to know what both of you will do if one of you is unwilling to continue dealing with this issue. If multiple attempts have been made at solving the problem and it still exists, this may be a good time to re-evaluate your relationship.

6. What else would you like to share on this topic?

This question is useful for couples seriously considering taking action in resolving a family conflict or who are already taking action. You can discuss your plans and make sure that both parties are on board before making any decisions.

7. Are there any ways you would like to improve our communication?

There are times when conflict arises due to poor communication between the couple, and extended family members become collateral damage. Sometimes, the best way to avoid getting into conflicts with family members is to talk about it with your partner first. If talking about family conflict does not work out, you may need professional help. Seeking a couple's counselor could be a good step forward in resolving disputes with your partner's relatives. The counselor can help you identify potential causes of conflict and how to deal with them once they arise.

8. How do you feel when we spend time together without your family members?

Some conflicts between families may be due to one partner feeling neglected by the other, or vice versa. Try doing fun activities with each other — without the interference of family — and see if your relationship improves. This will let you know if your partner is comfortable enough to spend quality time with just you. If the answer is no, perhaps you should try spending less time with his or her family and more time with each other.

9. What do you want to be said about our relationship with your family members?

Everyone wants to feel validated. Once you know that the topic of conversation is not going to end in an argument, it will be easier for both of you to talk and come up with a solution that will improve your relationship with extended family members.

10. What is the most important thing for both of us to remember when dealing with this issue?

This question is helpful if the conflict seems overwhelming and you both need something to take away from it. This way, if one or both of you forget about what was discussed after a while, talking about it again will be easier. After this conversation, hopefully you will have a better idea of how to mend your relationship with your partner's family members. If talking about it doesn't work out, you can see a couple's counselor to help improve communication and avoid future conflicts.

NOTES

Chapter 9:
Questions on Money Matters

G etting along with someone's financial habits can be just as important as getting along with them. Just like a couple has different tastes in food and music, they also might have different ideas about how they spend their money. Even in a relationship where both people earn an income, there is always the possibility that one person spends more than the other. This can be a sensitive area for some couples, and it can also cause resentment – and possibly even arguments! That's why it's important to talk about money issues together.

The next time you're together, find a place where you can have a conversation in private. Make sure that you have enough privacy to talk comfortably. If your partner is not very open about money issues, you might want to start off the conversation by asking what he or she thinks about money matters. Even if your partner is more open about their feelings on the subject, it can feel more natural if one person asks questions first.

If you want to have a friendly conversation about money, it can be helpful to have a few discussion points lined up. Here are some of the most important money topics that people might like to discuss:

1. What are your priorities when it comes to money?

This question will help you to understand what is important to your partner when it comes to spending and saving. A person's first answer might not be their final answer, so it is important to follow up with the following question:

2. How do you want to handle money as a couple?

If there are current habits you don't agree with, then it will be helpful to talk about how you can handle these differences moving forward. If the person you are dating has different spending habits than you, it is also helpful to talk about how much of an influence these differences might have on the future of the relationship.

3. Does my spending bother you?

This is a good question to ask if one of you is more frugal or spendthrift than the other. This could cause problems in the future, especially if one person likes to splurge and the other likes to save.

4. How can we work together on our money issues?

This helps both people understand how they can compromise moving forward. It also helps couple focus on only their money issues and not on other important relationship issues as well.

5. What are your financial goals?

It is a good idea for both partners in a relationship to have an understanding of each other's' financial goals, even if they are very different. If a couple has different goals, they should figure out how these goals will affect the relationship moving forward.

If you are dating someone you know casually, there are even more important issues to talk about. These include where each person sees their financial future in a year or two, and how much responsibility they want in the relationship. If both people earn money, it is also helpful to talk about who will be responsible for the household expenses.

These points might help your conversation along, or you can come up with other conversation points that are more relevant. The important thing is to have an open conversation and be honest with each other about your feelings on money matters.

The financial health of a household can be tied to the overall health of the relationship. Couples have a higher risk of divorce if they are neither financially satisfied nor financially compatible. One way to assess the health of a relationship is by looking at your credit reports, which provide a wealth of information about your relationship status and spending habits.

The lesson here: don't give yourself more credit than you deserve, and don't blow up your past or present successes out of proportion. Remember that you are just as fallible as your cohorts and future endeavors are no guarantee of success. Be patient with yourself and your money; try to be realistic in your expectations. It's easy to let the past determine the present and future.

That's why it's important not to compare yourself with others, especially when it comes to finances. The truth is that there really is no right or wrong way to handle money, and it's all about what works best for you. While there are always new methods of saving money coming out, the most important thing is to find what works best for you and your family. Here are more questions.

1. How would you describe our money situation? How do you feel about it?

2. Have there been any major changes in our finances recently? What caused them? Where do you hope they'll lead?

3. Are there things in your relationship that cause disagreements about money or make it difficult to talk about it?

4. What kind of help or advice do you want from regarding our money situation?

5. How can I support you financially?

6. Is there anything else we should discuss about our money situation?

If you have trouble talking to your partner about money, now is the time for a discussion! You might not always see eye-to-eye with your partner when it comes to financial decisions, but that doesn't mean that you shouldn't talk about the subject. After all, it is a very important thing in a relationship and needs to stay healthy for the relationship to stay healthy. If you're afraid to start a discussion about money because you don't know how to talk about it, try doing it in a fun way!

NOTES

Chapter 10:
Questions on Intimacy

Y es, intimacy is important! It's the foundation of our relationships and allows us to experience satisfying connections with the people we love. Intimacy is also a dynamic process that involves all of our senses: physical, emotional, intellectual, and spiritual. It means paying attention to what someone is saying while they are speaking, but also noticing their tone of voice, body language, and facial expressions.

Intimate communication goes beyond talking; in fact, it often happens through touch (like a hug or a kiss) or when we connect with someone "viscerally" by listening closely to their words and letting ourselves feel their emotions.

Intimacy isn't easy especially in the early stages of relationships. You may be wondering if you can really trust this person who seems so different from you. You'll need to be patient and open and take the time to get to know each other. If your partner wants the same thing, then intimacy can grow in the relationship, and may even get better over time.

If you want more intimacy in your relationship, you both need to be willing to share what turns you on as well as what turns you off; that is the only way you can truly find out what feels good for each partner. For instance, if he tells you that he enjoys watching pornography, or she reveals she has a foot fetish, those things may turn off or weird out a lot of people.

If you want to become more intimate, you need to be willing to reveal things you have a hard time talking about with just anyone (or maybe even at all). The more open and honest communication you can share, the closer you will feel.

However, giving and receiving intimacy is often a two-way street. If you want your partner to give of him or herself sexually, then in turn you need to be willing to open yourself up sexually as well. If your partner has sexual fantasies they would like fulfilled but won't ask for them, you need to be willing to fulfill their needs. It's important to have fun with each other, so have fun answering these questions! Ask them of each other.

1. When you think of me as your partner, what are the first things that come to mind? What associations do you have with me? What do I represent in your life? What do I mean to you and how so?

2. Were there moments when we were close to each other that you recall as being particularly special, romantic or intimate? Can you share those moments with me now? How did they make you feel?

3. In what ways have you been intimate that are important to you? Have there been times when you felt especially close to me?

4. What do you feel is the most important element of an intimate relationship? Is it sexual, emotional closeness, or something else? Why do you feel that way?

5. What are the differences in being intimate with a partner compared to a regular friendship? Are there differences in being intimate in a long-term relationship versus a new relationship or hooking up with someone for one night?

6. How often do you find yourselves not sharing enough "inner" things about yourself? What keeps you from being more open and vulnerable with me? At what points during our relationship have you felt especially open and intimate?

7. How much of your self-worth and sense of being has the relationship with me come to represent? What have been the most intense moments in our relationship?

8. What is it like for you to share something with me that you haven't told another person before? Be concrete. How does it feel? Are there things that you have tried not telling me, but I make you feel comfortable talking about?

9. How do different types of communication relate to intimacy: physical touch, sexual activities, intellectual connection, emotional sharing, spiritual connection?

10. What are the things that you do that allow for a deepening of intimacy? What do you need to do differently in order for the level of intimacy to grow for us?

11. How does the degree of intimacy in our relationship differ as a man and a woman? When does it work better? When is it worse?

12. What are good ways to introduce more emotional and physical closeness in our relationship? Be specific.

13. What are some of the challenges you have faced when trying to be more intimate in our interactions, in general and sexually?

14. How do you express your feelings about the closeness that we share?

15. What are some of the most intense moments in our relationship? Be concrete. How does it feel?

16. What has been most challenging about sharing sexual intimacy together? How can you overcome it?

17. Is there anything I have asked that made you feel nervous, uncomfortable, or a little self-conscious? Would you like to share with me what it was and why it made you feel that way?

18. Is there anything I have asked that you really liked talking about or being intimate with me? Would you like to share what that was and why it made you feel good?

19. Do you genuinely enjoy spending time together? What are some of your favorite activities together? What do you feel is important about doing these activities regularly with each another?

20. When you recall your best experiences in a relationship, what comes to mind? What are some of the most intense moments when you thinking back over the years at the beginning, middle and end of the relationship or a particular phase in it?

NOTES

Chapter 11:
Questions on Reconnecting with Your Spouse

T his chapter includes questions to get to know your partner better. They are designed to be used during personal time together. If you choose to answer them all, consider spending 30 minutes talking about the questions one night a week for 6 weeks. Or if you choose to only answer a few, consider picking questions you would like to work on for the coming week and talking about them at a time that works best for both. Make sure you are in a quiet place where the two of you can sit comfortably. Read the questions (there is one for each of you) and ask each other the questions in order. Discuss what was said and how you feel about it. You don't have to answer all the questions at once. You can pick the ones you want to work on together.

Here we go!

In your relationship, it's important to be open with each other and share things about yourself that you wouldn't share with others. Take turns answering and try not to hold back! If it makes you uncomfortable, that's a good thing because sharing feelings may help you both better understand each other.

1. What is one physical thing that you love about yourself?

This question is designed to help you understand what your partner likes about his/her body. Some of you are probably thinking, "I'm happy with my body," or something similar. If so, ask the follow-up question: what one physical thing would you like to change about yourself? (You could say, "What's one thing you'd like to change about your appearance?") This will get both of you thinking and talking about physical attributes.

2. How is our sex life?

This question is designed to further tap into feelings that may be difficult for both of you to talk about. Try to relax and share what you feel. If you are uncomfortable with the question, think about what things in the bedroom could be improved. If you choose to answer this question together, it may be helpful to answer what do we do that you like but I don't? Could we try that?

3. What do I do that frustrates / annoys / bothers you?

The purpose of this question is to identify frustrations in the relationship so they can be addressed and worked on. This will also give you insight into your spouse's personality and help the two of you become closer by becoming more understanding of each other. For example, if you find out that being late frustrates your spouse, arrange to leave early or have more communication about the plan ahead of time.

4. Do I do things that have made you proud?

Many of you are probably thinking, "Yes! Of course!" But there's a great truth in this question: if your spouse made you proud for doing something in the past, then he/she will continue to do so in the future! It is important to understand what your spouse thinks is a win-win situation and what makes him/her feel good about himself/herself as well as the relationship.

5. What do I need to be more comfortable around you?

This question is designed to get you talking about things that might be uncomfortable. For many of you, it will touch on sexual feelings. Don't be afraid to share "intimate" feelings with each other. Remember that the point of this book is to have a loving and intimate relationship in which you are comfortable sharing your inner thoughts and desires.

6. What are some things I can do for you that will have an impact on your life?

This question is designed to help us all think about how we can make a positive difference. We want our spouses to feel like they can count on us and that we truly care about them. It is important we do things to show our support. What are some things that your spouse does that have made a positive impact on your life? What would you like them to do in the future?

7. What would you never want me to do?

This question is designed to help you think about boundaries in the relationship and respecting those boundaries. There may be something you want to do, but because of your spouse's personality or past experiences, it might not be something he/she feels good about. This is an important area for discussion. It's better that those feelings come up now than later when both of you have invested more in the relationship.

8. What would you do if I got fired from my job?

This question is designed to provoke feelings and thoughts about what life would be like if one of you were not in the same place. This can be a difficult question for some because it deals with an unpleasant subject that might cause feelings of sadness, fear, or guilt. It is good to talk about these things now so that you understand each other's reactions and plans ahead of time.

9. What's your happiest memory with me?

This question is designed to help you focus on positive memories from the past, present, and future. It is important to identify the things that made your relationship stronger in the past, as well as the things that will make your relationship stronger in the future. Even though this is a tough question, try not to be negative when talking about the memories you have. It is important to remember that even though people change over time, your love for each other should not change.

This brings us back to the importance of communicating in a positive way and remembering our love for one another.

10. How did I make you feel during _____ (a past experience)?

This question is designed to get you thinking about how you can communicate with each other better in the future by learning from past experiences. It is important to remember that you have different communication styles. It may be that in the past, your spouse reacted in a negative way to something you did because his/her communication style was different than yours. You want to learn about each other's communication styles so you can talk about things in an effective manner going forward.

After going through these 10 questions, it is good to go back and focus on the first one. You should be able to remember what your spouse said to you in response to each of the 10 questions. This will make it easier for you both to communicate with each other going forward. It is important for you to remember that by doing this exercise, there was a deeper level of communication and understanding between you. You were able to talk about things that can be uncomfortable for some couples and were still able to have a good, positive conversation about them. This kind of communication will help your relationship grow stronger from this point forward.

NOTES

Chapter 12:
Day-to-day Conflict Resolution

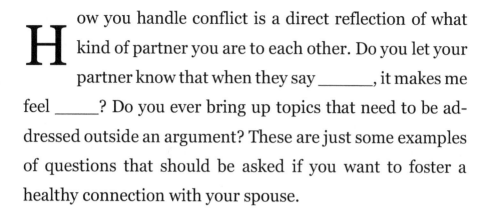

How you handle conflict is a direct reflection of what kind of partner you are to each other. Do you let your partner know that when they say _____, it makes me feel _____? Do you ever bring up topics that need to be addressed outside an argument? These are just some examples of questions that should be asked if you want to foster a healthy connection with your spouse.

This book explores 10 important questions for couples and offers insights on how to answer them. Trust is the foundation of a healthy relationship. Do you know if your partner has an online presence? Is he or she active on social media? As with everything, check the comments for any signs of negativity.

When couples have the same vision of what they want to achieve together, their dreams are more likely to be realized. For example, if one partner wants to start a business or buys a house and the other is unwilling (or has different plans), then that partnership may dissolve. Firmly aligning your goals in life will help you make decisions together as a couple.

These are just some examples of the questions that should be asked if you want to foster a healthy connection with your spouse. You already know how important communication is in any relationship. It is the foundations of all good relationships, and it applies whether you're married or not.

Remember that when answering these questions, honesty is always the best policy, and when in doubt, err on the side of carefully considering your words.

It's normal for partners to disagree sometimes (even married couples). With this question, ask yourself whether you find yourself falling into that trap often. If so, it may be valuable to have a conversation about how to approach conflict more effectively in the future.

If your partner constantly brings up past mistakes (or yours), it may be time to talk about how to approach the subject differently. A relationship is a living thing, and it's important to nurture it properly.

How do you feel when you get in fights? Are they draining? Does it seem like you're repeating yourself? Do you have confidence that your partner is listening to what you say (even if he or she doesn't agree)? These questions should be discussed. Ask yourself if your goals in life are compatible with your partner's.

This applies to both short-term and long-term goals. For example, if one partner decides to take a year off from school, the other might not be on board with that decision. As a result, problems arise when one is trying to move forward and the other is trying to hold him or her back.

If you have different visions of what you want in 10 years, then talk it out. Maybe your partner wants children, and you want a career. Maybe your partner wants to live on the beach, and you want to live in the mountains. As long as both partners understand each other's life dreams, then they're more likely to come together and decide on a compromise that works for both of them.

Conclusion

There are many ways to communicate in a loving relationship. As an example, consider the "no contact" rule. It basically dictates that partners must separate themselves from each other during arguments or other intense discussions and not initiate or accept contact until they have cooled off. If this rule is not followed, much harm can be caused to the relationship, especially if the argument escalates to physical violence.

It is also important that people understand why they argue with their partners in the first place. It helps them realize what could be causing conflict within their relationship and what they can do to work together to fix it before it gets worse. There is a vast array of methods to resolve conflicts, from mediation to couples counseling. Whatever route people decide to take, it is extremely important that they are aware of the potential consequences. If not, a small disagreement could escalate into something more serious.

It is also important for partners to remember that there are some things that can never be solved. If this happens, it is best to learn how to carry on with life without dwelling on the argument as if there is no hope of a resolution. This will allow them to avoid getting caught up in the conflict and possibly causing further harm to the relationship as a result of their refusal to compromise.

The whole point of communication is for couples to understand each other and work out differences together rather than losing patience or taking sides against one another.

The list of 20 questions provided aims to help couples understand and appreciate each other, talk about their feelings, listen to each other more and share their thoughts.

These questions are for all types of relationships - same gender or others, married or not married. We also encourage you to use the answers as a starting point for discussions about things not included in this list.

Thank you.